ROC

COOKING SPACES

DESIGNS FOR COOKING, ENTERTAINING, AND LIVING

HELEN THOMPSON   ANNA KASABIAN, CONTRIBUTING WRITER

ROCKPORT PUBLISHERS

To my husband, Charles Lohrmann, whose ideas about what goes on in a kitchen

give me—an undistinguished chef—hope that it isn't all about cooking.

© 2000 by Rockport Publishers, Inc.
First paperback edition printed in 2002

First published in the United States of America by

Rockport Publishers, Inc.

33 Commercial Street

Gloucester, Massachusetts 01930-5089

Telephone: (978) 282-9590

Fax: (978) 283-2742

www.rockpub.com

ISBN 1-56496-888-X

10 9 8 7 6 5 4 3 2 1

Design: Leeann Leftwich

Cover Image: Andrew Wood, The Interior Archive

Back Cover Photo: Mike Paul

Printed in China.

Contents

The Kitchen as a Gathering Place

92

Kitchen Traditions

116

introduction

KITCHENS ARE ABOUT COOKING—or so I feared when I was asked to write this book. Of course I worried that my solipsistic culinary skills would completely undermine the book's credibility. I was also concerned that I would quickly be exposed to the world for the pathetic cook my friends know me to be.

However, I soon realized that I was not being asked to write a cookbook. I would be writing, rather, a book about kitchens. And the more I thought about kitchens, particularly kitchens I have known and loved, the more apparent it became that so much of what makes a kitchen a cooking space has very little to do with how virtuosic the cook is. In fact, hovering gently in my adult psyche are memories of our family kitchen, the scene of pre-school breakfasts of sugar-saturated shredded wheat—the slightly soggy, bristly pillows of wheat shards floating in milk will never be classified as respectable cooking. But I liked casually pulverizing the cereal before I consumed it and I liked eating breakfast with my parents. I also liked the kitchen—it had casement windows that overlooked a patio—because it was full of music from the resident radio, it was where my father shined his shoes, and it was where my mother's college friend Mary Ann offered me a glimpse of the spectacular red crinoline petticoat she wore under a huge swirl of a skirt. Of course, we convened in the kitchen three times a day for meals, but oddly my memories are much more about what went on in the kitchen than of specific meals consumed.

I think that my experience is not unusual. In fact, the conversations had with chefs included in this book are full of reminiscences as much about objects, place, and time as about food. And, once my editors and I divided the book into chapters, it was obvious that cooking was only a component of what goes on in the most important room in the house.

In my research for the book I discovered that kitchens evolved from places that were physically separate from the house and its goings on to places that, though incorporated into a residential building, were nevertheless psychologically removed from the household's activities. A kitchen's placement in the house had little to do with food, and a lot to do with how the homeowner—and society at large—regarded cooking and serving food. Once safety issues were resolved thanks to appliances more modern than an open fire, kitchens became very social. They even became places where new ideas—about efficiency and subsequently, design—could be tested and asserted.

The kitchens in *Cooking Spaces* reveal a range of ideas about how this part of a house should function. Some spaces are emphatically for cooking, with gleaming, industrial-strength appliances occupying center stage. Others are barely there, with functionality so effectively hidden behind sleek cabinetry that only the profile of the sink's faucet tattles the truth about the room's purpose. I found this vast array of ideas energizing. There is no other room in the house that has inspired so much thought. There is no other room in the house that reveals so clearly the evolution of family life.

It is a heartening sign that houses today have a main room, and it's not the living room. Much in modern life contributes to the fracturing of family life, but one trend does not. It's a good sign that these days, the kitchen has become the heart of the house.

kitchens that work

A GOOD COOK CAN BE A GOOD COOK ALMOST ANYWHERE.

BUT A WELL-DESIGNED KITCHEN CAN TRANSFORM A GOOD COOK INTO A GREAT COOK.

Cooking spaces that work make life easier, whether you are an ambitious home chef or a busy professional who dines on take-out food. The first step to an efficient kitchen is to think about your cooking lifestyle, how you use your kitchen, whether for quick meals or large family gatherings (see Cooking Lifestyle Quiz on next page). Start by deciding what you will be doing in your new kitchen, and then calculate how much time you will want to spend in the kitchen. As simple as this reconsideration sounds, it is basic to producing a successful kitchen that responds to your needs—going back to the fundamentals is the key to an efficient kitchen.

There are five functions that a well-planned kitchen must make room for: storage, food preparation, cooking, eating, and clean-up. Assess your needs in each of these areas to determine which are the strong points in the dynamics of your kitchen. If you use lots of fresh foods—instead of planning, preparing, and freezing dinners days in advance—opt for cool, well-ventilated storage for vegetables and fruits. Make sure that you have enough refrigerator, freezer, and cabinet space to accommodate your choice of cooking ingredients. Allow space for cooking equipment as well as items you purchase in bulk, such as large packages, cans, and bottles, and arrange storage for easy access—frequently used items should be kept somewhere between knee height and eye level.

LEFT As ingenuous as a child's building blocks, the space-defining blue cabinets seem to have rolled into this high-ceilinged room. They make an arresting look in a low-budget cooking area.

RIGHT Translucent blue Plexiglas is inexpensive but its visual impact shows how much can be achieved with imaginative use of the ordinary.

Enough work space for food preparation demands careful planning and a long, hard look at the kinds of food you prepare, the number of people you cook for, and whether you share the food-prep spaces with others. Think about how you like to cook—a chef with a preference for elaborate entertaining will need equipment that is different from the cook who likes to re-heat convenience foods. Consider, also, ventilation systems, double ovens, or a heavy-duty range if you frequently prepare large meals. Where you like to eat or to serve food will help you decide how multipurpose your space will be. If you like to serve large meals in the kitchen, allow space for a large table with a good source of natural light, in a draft-free area away from the main cooking activity.

If you have children, a bar area for quick meals may be your best option. For small spaces, a banquette or window seat will free up room for extra seating. The bane of many a cook's existence is clean-up, which doesn't have to be onerous if adequate space is allotted. Make dishwashing and food recycling simple by choosing the sink, drainage space, and dishwasher based on the amount of work you do. Even if this is an unglamorous aspect of cooking, do not stint on the space needed to do the job right.

Kitchens are also about those elements that aren't quantifiable. Poor lighting, overcrowding, inefficient storage, and inconvenient spaces are all-too-common problems in most kitchens—but they are often just the quixotic features that give a room its personality. Ingenuity can do more to

THE FIRST STEP IN DETERMINING HOW TO MAKE YOUR KITCHEN WORK IS TO ANSWER SOME BASIC LIFESTYLE QUESTIONS. ARMED WITH THE ANSWERS TO THESE QUESTIONS, YOU CAN CREATE THE BEST, MOST PRACTICAL ARRANGEMENTS FOR EVERY INCH OF YOUR KITCHEN.

• DO YOU OFTEN COOK AND ENTERTAIN AT HOME? WHEN YOU DO, IS IT INTIMATE SUPPERS FOR A COUPLE OR A FAMILY GATHERING OF FOUR TO SIX PEOPLE, OR DO YOU COOK GRAND DINNERS FOR LARGE FAMILY GATHERINGS AND PARTIES?

• ARE YOU ONE-HALF OF A PROFESSIONAL COUPLE WHO DINES ON EASY-TO-MAKE PASTA AND SALAD MEALS, PRE-PREPARED FOODS, OR TAKE-OUT DINNERS?

• HOW MANY PEOPLE PREPARE FOOD AND COOK IN YOUR KITCHEN? WHAT OTHER ACTIVITIES TAKE PLACE IN YOUR KITCHEN?

• DO YOU HAVE ANY PHYSICAL AILMENTS, SUCH AS BACK PAIN, THAT LIMIT YOUR ACCESS TO POTS AND PANS?

• WHAT ARE YOUR BUYING HABITS? DO YOU PURCHASE AND STORE MOSTLY FRESH FOOD, OR TEND TO COLLECT CANNED AND FROZEN FOODS?

• ARE YOU A CONNOISSEUR OF FINE WINES?

LEFT Undeterred by the fact that this kitchen isn't technically big enough to accommodate both an island and an eating area, the designer achieved a sense of spaciousness by adding legs to an otherwise blocky island and leaving the shelving open. The table wraps around the end of the island, providing just enough dining space for guests.

ABOVE Green is the most soothing of colors (remember that many hospitals believe this theory), and its soft hue is a peaceful contrast to the stainless-steel appliances and cabinetry.

bring a kitchen to life than all the smart appliances in the world. Ingenious solutions to design flaws are, after all, the reason some of the world's greatest chefs and kitchen designers came to love cooking—and to love their kitchens.

Food historian Burt Wolf, author of the now-classic *The Cooks' Catalog*, likes to relate an experience he once had with coauthor Beard at a cooking demonstration the two were giving at a famous department store. When Beard attempted to turn on the store's stovetop, he discovered that the burners weren't working. Ever enterprising, the great dean of American cooking retrieved ten clothing irons from the nearby household-appliances department and proceeded to prepare an entire meal of tiny pancakes, steamed brocolli, and chicken medallions—with steam-iron heat.

As Beard so serendipitously proved, a cook can get away with less-than-adequate equipment. But, most of us would rather not, and we probably don't have ten steam irons handy anyway. We prefer to be well-equipped culinarily—and more so now than ever. Sometimes, unfortunately, we find our kitchens coming up a little short, although probably not as dramatically as Beard's near disaster.

ABOVE Because the kitchen tends to be the center of household management, it makes sense to set off an area for a home office where you can pay bills, plan menus, and structure budgets, and still keep an eye on the surrounding activities.

RIGHT Color can do several things at once. In a neutral-hued small house or apartment, it can separate one space from another. It can also make something ordinary, such as a kitchen sink, special. The pristine blue tile sink surround becomes an important design element in this tiny kitchen.

OPPOSITE Conventional wisdom would probably discourage positioning a cabinet directly in front of a window, but in this oddly shaped kitchen there isn't much choice. Instead of a hindrance, the window becomes an anchor for the cabinet, and important storage—lost because of the wall angle—is regained with a long bar for pots and pans.

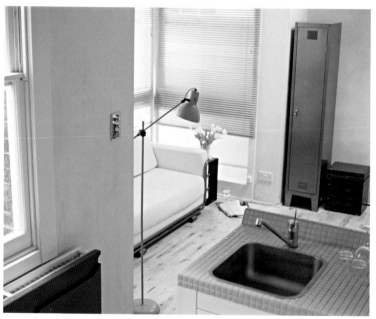

JACQUES PEPIN IS THE
CELEBRATED HOST OF AWARD-WINNING COOK-
ING SHOWS ON NATIONAL PUBLIC TELEVISION,
A MASTER CHEF, FOOD COLUMNIST, COOKING
TEACHER, AND AUTHOR OF NINETEEN COOK-
BOOKS. IN THE EARLY YEARS OF HIS CAREER, HE
WAS THE PERSONAL CHEF TO THREE FRENCH
HEADS OF STATE, INCLUDING CHARLES DE GAULLE.

PEPIN WRITES A QUARTERLY COLUMN FOR
FOOD AND WINE AND IS A POPULAR GUEST ON
GOOD MORNING AMERICA, THE TODAY SHOW,
AND *THE LATE SHOW WITH DAVID LETTERMAN.*
MR. PEPIN'S NEWEST VENTURE IS A TWENTY-
TWO-SHOW SERIES WITH JULIA CHILD ENTITLED
JULIA AND JACQUES COOKING AT HOME. HE
ALSO AUTHORED A COMPANION BOOK OF THE
SAME TITLE.

*JACQUE PEPIN'S KITCHEN: ENCORE WITH
CLAUDINE,* ANOTHER PBS-TV SERIES, THE SEC-
OND FEATURING HIS DAUGHTER CLAUDINE,
WAS NAMED BEST NATIONAL TV COOKING
SHOW AT THE JAMES BEARD AWARDS IN 1999.
THE FIRST TWENTY-SIX-SHOW SEASON OF THIS
SERIES, ENTITLED *JACQUES PEPIN'S KITCHEN:
COOKING WITH CLAUDINE,* WAS A JAMES
BEARD AWARD WINNER IN 1997.

When Jacques Pepin was a little boy in France, his family's kitchen was bombed three times—"first by the Americans, then the Italians, and then the Germans. It was a small apartment, one of eight or ten in a building, and it was close to the railroad tracks, which is why it kept getting bombed!" At the time his mother was a waitress and his father was a carpenter.

The next three kitchens Pepin had in his life were in the restaurants his mother and father owned. To help out, he would feed the chickens, tend the garden, wash wine bottles, string the beans, and peel potatoes. "From the moment we had the restaurant it was my 'home' kitchen. Our first restaurant kitchen was open and had a big, square wooden table. There was a window over the sink, and a wood stove. It was a very pleasant room and was the place where we came to sit and eat."

His family's second restaurant was in a suburb of Lyon, and Pepin's duties here included raking the boules (similar to a boci court) and bringing wine and drinks to customers. "That second kitchen was a bit more sophisticated. There was a big stove, and I remember it had a tile floor and walls.

"The third restaurant kitchen had a coal-burning stove and there was a reservoir to do the dishes. And there was a stairway from the kitchen to the upstairs where we slept." This was a small, family restaurant where Pepin recalls customers coming right into the kitchen, lifting the pot tops, and smelling the food. "They'd say, 'This is what I want to eat.' The regulars came in every day, a week, or month at a time."

Pepin's daily ritual involved going to the market with his mother on the way to school, and then accompanying her after school to carry her purchases to the restaurant. At age thirteen, Pepin began his apprenticeship at the Hotel de l'Europe in Bourg-en-Brasse. "This was a big, beautiful hotel, and the kitchen was all tile, from the floor to the ceiling. There were big windows, and the roof was stained glass. Big French doors allowed clientele to stop and watch us cook, and there was a wood stove. Running the stove was its own apprenticeship." He had to learn how to heat it up, and maintain a steady heat. "If you're in charge of the stove, and it goes lukewarm, you'd get killed!"

Today, Jacques Pepin's Connecticut kitchen (his house used to be a small brick factory!) is his own creation, customized to fulfill his every cooking need. "The kitchen accommodates our psychological and utilitarian needs. It is a very large room, and is open to the dining room and living room, 30 by 40 feet, and has a center island with a granite top that is 9 feet by 5 feet. The whole inside of the island is filled with cabinets."

"To me the first thing a kitchen has to be is functional, then you make it look good! There is a big wall covered with driftwood and the wood is covered with pots. It's probably 12 feet high and 15 feet wide, with one hundred pots—copper, cast iron, enamel, aluminum—all useful, none are here for decoration."

The room has big windows, which give him a view of the pond and guesthouse on the property. It also has two dishwashers, a Viking gas stove with a grill, a two-burner Gaggeneau, two wall ovens, and an outside kitchen, which has a big wood oven and a grill. "We entertain a lot," he says, explaining the need for all the cooking areas.

Pepin has chosen natural wood tones for the cabinetry, but the look is old rather than sleek and new, and his walls are white and blue tile. On one wall, his own tile creation, which resembles a Matisse, depicts an open window with a seascape and his own drawings are featured on hand-painted tiles. "There's a chicken, a fish, a radish, a leek—so the kitchen is very personalized."

To keep his collection of about forty knives in easy reach, he had custom slits cut into the granite countertop. "Where the blade goes is a short drawer, [where] I have paper towel, plastic wrap, and aluminum foil. Under that drawer on the tiled floor I have a rolling garbage can, so it's a very functional area."

The lesson for us all in James Beard's improvisation is that a good cook can be a good cook almost anywhere—great kitchens aren't always the ones that are picture-perfect. Many, in fact, are full of flaws or are idiosyncratic, but are miraculously workable nevertheless. In fact, the so-called "flaws" our kitchens possess may actually be what endears them to us: the British kitchen designer, Johnny Grey has developed a brilliant career creating eccentric and colorful "unfitted" kitchens because of his fond memories of the kitchen in the house where he grew up. Small and chaotic, the kitchen was the place where his mother cooked and the family of seven ate their meals. But here, life and laughter bubbled into a heady atmosphere that has stayed with Grey all his life. His designs—oversized, freestanding pantries; curvaceous painted islands; and unabashedly mismatched cabinets—attest to the vitality that kitchens should bring to a house.

The choice to keep certain less-than-ideal aspects of a kitchen can also be deliberate. Dominique Browning, the editor of *House & Garden* magazine, recalls the warmth of her grandparents' kitchen in Kentucky, where she often visited as a child. Her grandfather steadfastly refused to modernize the room, and in particular, he refused to get a dishwasher. But his reason was not one of obstinacy—rather, he claimed that there was nothing he liked better than standing beside his wife as she washed the dishes and handing a dish to her, one by one, for her to dry and put away. Good kitchens aren't always about efficiency—but they are always about the elements that make a home function well, and happily.

Make an ordinary kitchen into a cooking space by infusing it with elements of your personality and style.

the **smart** kitchen

The average kitchen is as busy as any office, so when you're planning a new or renovated cooking space, think carefully about how and what you *organize* and store in it. List the *present contents of your kitchen:* Dishes (drinking glasses, cups, bowls, and plates), everyday flatware, cooking utensils, pots and pans, specialty pans, small countertop appliances, microwave bowls and plates, plastic storage containers, dry food, canned goods, bottled water, juices, paper goods, cleaning supplies, recycling bin (separating paper and glass), and trash bin. From this list, consider the various items that you need to keep in short- and long-term storage, from the extra containers of bottled water, to the plastic food containers that keep food fresh in the refrigerator, to your formal silverware and linens. Then make a wish list for the best location of each of these items, whether in a wall or floor cabinet, open shelves, drawers, or mobile storage. You don't have to group together like items, such as all pans and pots in the same area; consider gathering in one large drawer all of the pots you typically use in a week's worth of preparing dinner. Plan storage according to how you work in your *cooking space,* and your kitchen will become a well-organized cooking machine.

Keep often-used pots within reach of the stove and oven. A cluster of pots hanging above a counter is both easy to reach and visually interesting. Do not suspend pots directly above a stovetop, as grease and dust collect more easily on the pots.

Arrange storage for easy access. Frequently used items should be kept somewhere between knee height and eye level.

Think vertically as well as horizontally. Incorporate vertical slots in a cabinet near an oven to store large flat baking pans and cutting boards.

For an attractive and practical way to display and keep everyday dishes, stack them in open shelves above the countertop. This arrangement works best if the dishes are used and washed daily; if not, store them in glass-fronted cabinets, which prevent dust collection yet show off the colors and patterns of your dishes.

A stove hood can easily become a major design element in the kitchen. Although some cooks prefer the extra headroom a downdraft system installed at the back of a stovetop allows, a stove without a hood often looks bereft.

ABOVE Ideally, what could be more efficient than a kitchen where a cook can stand in one place and get everything done? Even though this streamlined cooking space is just half a galley kitchen, everything is within reach, and a place to eat is just steps away. Space has been maximized, but not at the expense of looks.

OPPOSITE Store utensils in the area they'll be used the most.

JODY ADAMS A NATIVE OF
PROVIDENCE, RHODE ISLAND, CHEF JODY
ADAMS HAS RECEIVED KUDOS FOR HER IMAGI-
NATIVE COOKING FROM INTERNATIONAL AND
LOCAL PRESS. HER FORMAL COOKING CAREER
BEGAN IN 1983 WHEN SHE WORKED UNDER
LYDIA SHIRE AT THE SEASONS IN BOSTON.
FROM THERE, SHE MOVED TO HAMERSLEY'S
BISTRO AS A SOUS CHEF, AND THEN TO
MICHELA'S IN 1990 WHERE SHE HELD THE
TITLE EXECUTIVE CHEF. IN 1994, SHE OPENED
RIALTO WITH RESTAURATEURS AND PARTNERS
MICHELA LARSON AND KAREN HASKELL. SHE
LIVES IN SOMERVILLE, MASSACHUSETTS,
WITH HER HUSBAND KEN AND THEIR TWO
CHILDREN, OLIVER AND ROXANNE.

Food, cooking, and the kitchen have been an integral part of Jody Adams' life from the time she was a little girl. She has fond memories of her grandmother's kitchen, and remembers sitting around an old pine table that was nearly white as snow from being cleaned by bleach. It wasn't a fancy kitchen, and there was barely any counter space. "I remember [the kitchen] had this wonderful maroon-colored countertop and matching linoleum floors. She kept a huge freezer, and the back hall was cold, and that's where she would store things she bought from the farmer's market...and it always smelled like leg of lamb!"

She and her family lived in England for a year, and the stove in her friend's house, named Bessie, is one she never forgot. "It was a fabulous stove; on all the time. It ran with wood or charcoal and had different compartments. It heated the house, cooked the food, and dried the clothes."

When Adams was growing up, the most important thing in her family, she says, was sitting around the table together for meals. "We had candles, and it was a warm and friendly place to congregate. It was really important that we all be there. And we always had homemade food; nothing was ever frozen or packaged," she says. As for the design, the kitchen was a long, narrow, functional, basic space with a breakfast table, and "we had the same appliances forever."

Jody's mother was the primary cook in the family, but her father always cooked Sunday breakfast—his specialty was cornmeal pancakes. His other specialty was homemade mayonnaise, and that was a regular addition to the coleslaw served each Thanksgiving.

"My mother was adventurous, and followed the recipes of Elizabeth David, whose cookbooks she collected. She loved to entertain, and my sister and I ultimately participated in that—setting the table and clearing, and eventually, we cooked. So we were being caterers!"

And through all this Adams began to notice that while her parents' parties ended up in the dining room, the kitchen was the place to be. "What I learned very early on was that no matter how small the kitchen is, people are always there—that's where the fun was."

While an anthropology major at Brown University, she took a part-time job working for Nancy Verde Barr, a food writer and teacher. That job would change the course of her life. Her interest in anthropology was quickly overshadowed by a growing passion for food and the kitchen.

After graduating from Brown, Adams traveled to Spain and Portugal. It was there, she says, that she learned another important lesson about cooking. "I was at a youth hostel, and bought some fish from a fisherman, and came back to my room to cook it on one burner. It was such a delicious meal...so the perfect kitchen is really just what's happening at the moment. You can make the most delicious memorable meal without the gadgets."

Today, she and her husband are in the middle of planning the renovation for their kitchen, and she is testing recipes for a new cookbook.

Jody's ideal kitchen would have an old feeling as opposed to slick, a couch so people could "sit and hang out," pleasant light, and functional surfaces. "Right now we have a stainless-steel prep table and metro shelving, like you would have in a restaurant kitchen. But in renovating, I'd like wooden cupboards with a warmer feeling. I don't want anything fancy, or cutting edge.

"What is most important is that it is a functional space where I don't worry about ruining anything. I like having a stainless-steel counter so I can put down a hot pan and not worry about burning a surface. And I would love to have a drain in the middle of the floor!"

Other requirements for Ms. Adams are a gas stove with more than four burners, a stovetop grill, two refrigerators, two ovens, plenty of sink space, and a view wherever most of the work is going on.

"A fireplace would be nice," she adds, "lots of cutting boards, and a place to hang my pots. I'd have my equipment accessible like it is in the restaurant. There would be a stainless-steel table for my Cuisinart and Kitchen Aid."

Upholstered yellow
steel-frame chairs are
a soft contrast to the
stainless-steel kitchen
and table.

ABOVE A bland kitchen was inexpensively revitalized with color and open shelving, two design elements that are eye-catching and within reach of any budget.

OPPOSITE It is always easy to assemble a kitchen, but the secret is to improvise. Don't just settle for the ordinary, such as stock cabinets; scour junk and salvage shops, restaurant-supply companies, and auctions for furniture and accessories that can be adapted to kitchen use.

cooks' kitchens

MRS. ISABELLA BEETON, THE MARTHA STEWART OF HER TIME AND AUTHOR OF *THE BOOK OF HOUSEHOLD MANAGEMENT*, STATED EMPHATICALLY IN THE 1861 PUBLICATION THAT THE KITCHEN IS THE "GREAT LABORATORY OF THE HOUSEHOLD."

In the sense that this room is where all the "labor" that kept the household running took place, Mrs. Beeton's characterization of the kitchen hasn't changed that much. But what has changed is that kitchens—once so labor-intensive—now strive to be labor saving. Part of the reason is that now there is usually one cook, maybe two, in a household. In Mrs. Beeton's time there may have been a staff, and no one—aside from the cooks themselves—was terribly concerned about the efficiency of their laboratory.

Times have changed, and now kitchens must also be efficient. Serious cooks will have it no other way, whether they are cooking just for themselves, for family, or as a profession. In fact, many so-called modern ideas for residential kitchens originated at work—but not necessarily the cooking profession. In the twenties and thirties, new kitchen design elaborated on discoveries made by efficiency experts trying to improve performance on assembly lines. By separating work areas, production proliferated. This translated into separate areas for washing, preparation, storage, and cooking in the residential kitchen.

Today, the biggest breakthrough in kitchen design—and it is a deceptively simple one—is continued workspace. The efficiency experts of the twenties and thirties extolled the value of separate work areas, which accommodated well when there was more than one cook in the kitchen. But you know the adage about too many cooks, and it is particularly applicable in modern kitchens. With work areas chopped up into separate staging arenas, a single person can waste much precious cooking time running from station to station. Preparation, cooking, and clean-up goes better if there is connecting space.

OPPOSITE Islands are the workhorse of the kitchen and are worth having even if it means reconfiguring space to fit them in. They offer well-organized storage and a roomy work surface for everything from meal prep to informal dining—and they are always a handy spot for friends to gather around. Islands work best when unencumbered by appliances; with legs, they appear lighter and less blocky.

FOLLOWING PAGE A hard-working kitchen doesn't have to have a lot of showy gadgets on display. To get the most out of your cooking space, choose elements that answer questions of form and function. Even with just the basics—task lighting, some storage, a table, a stove, a sink, and a refrigerator—a well-designed kitchen can be endowed with stunning minimalist style.

Serious cooks, though, probably don't dream about connecting space. Their fantasies are inhabited by restaurant-style ranges, 15,000-BTU cooktops, gleaming stainless-steel appliances, maple butcher-block counters, and copper pots and pans shining on racks overhead. But deep in their hearts—and very close to their pocketbooks—is the reality check that all these expensive gew gaws mean nothing if the kitchen's layout isn't functional.

Ideas about efficiency vary depending on culinary specialty. If baking is what you do, then the ideal kitchen will include stone surfaces; plenty of storage for trays, pans, and utensils; shoulder-height ovens; and a dedicated place for mixers and other tools of the trade. A vegetarian cook will be looking for a kitchen with loads of storage—both for refrigerated foods and non-perishable items.

In this section, we have looked to the professionals—caterers, chefs, and food testers—for suggestions about how kitchens work best. Their ideas are based on years of research and experience, and—fancy appliances aside—when food tastes great it is because there is a happy cook in the kitchen. After all, a cook's kitchen is really all about efficiency and about the way the cook expects to function.

ABOVE Adding a second stovetop for specialty cooking, such as grilling or broiling, is realistic for serious and frequent meal preparation.

OPPOSITE Even stainless steel isn't indestructible. For tough cutting projects, keep a slab of marble handy to prevent scarring and scratching steel countertops.

KITCHEN TIPS

EQUIP LOW-VOLTAGE, SUSPENDED LIGHTS WITH DIMMER SWITCHES TO GIVE USERS CONTROL OVER THE ROOM'S LIGHTING.

SQUARED-OFF EDGES BLOCK PATHWAYS: ROUND OFF KITCHEN ISLANDS AND CABINET EDGES, SO THAT THEIR CURVES FORM A KIND OF SOFT GEOMETRY AND MAKE THE KITCHEN APPEAR MORE USER-FRIENDLY.

PLACE THE ISLAND IN THE MIDDLE OF THE ROOM SO THAT THE COOK CAN INTERACT WITH FAMILY MEMBERS AND GUESTS. INCORPORATE STOVE BURNERS, WORK COUNTERS OF VARYING HEIGHTS, AND A SMALL-APPLIANCE COUNTER SO THAT KEY ACTIVITIES CAN BE FOCUSED IN ONE AREA. ALSO INCLUDE A COUPLE OF BARSTOOLS SO THAT FAMILY AND FRIENDS CAN SIT AND CHAT WITH THE COOK.

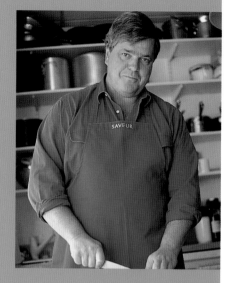

COLMAN ANDREWS

IS THE EDITOR OF *SAVEUR* AND THE AUTHOR OF THREE ACCLAIMED BOOKS ON FOOD: *EVERYTHING ON THE TABLE, FLAVORS OF THE RIVIERA,* AND *CATALAN CUISINE.* IN ADDITION, HE IS THE COAUTHOR AND COEDITOR OF *SAVEUR COOKS AUTHENTIC AMERICAN* AND *SAVEUR COOKS AUTHENTIC FRENCH.* HE IS A REGULAR GUEST CHEF ON NBC'S *TODAY SHOW,* AND HAS APPEARED ON *GOOD MORNING AMERICA,* THE FOOD NETWORK, THE LIFETIME CHANNEL, AND THE DISCOVERY CHANNEL, AMONG OTHERS.

AMONG ANDREWS' MANY WRITING AWARDS IS THE 1999 BEST AMERICAN COOKBOOK AWARD AND BEST FEATURE WRITING WITH RECIPES AWARD. A FORMER RESTAURANT REVIEWER AND RESTAURANT NEWS COLUMNIST FOR THE *LOS ANGELES TIMES,* HE HAS BEEN WRITING ON THE TOPICS OF FOOD, WINE, AND THE ARTS SINCE 1968. HIS BYLINE HAS APPEARED IN *METROPOLITAN HOME,* AMONG OTHER PUBLICATIONS. HE WAS ONE OF THE FIRST FIFTY AMERICAN FOOD AND WINE FIGURES TO BE NAMED IN *WHO'S WHO OF COOKING IN AMERICA.*

When Colman Andrews was growing up in Los Angeles, California, the kitchen was big, with lots of empty space. Actually, it was most perfect, he says for skating in his socks. "Now designers pay a lot of attention to the triangle of the refrigerator, sink, and stove, but this had lots of empty space. My mother was not a good cook, so maybe that space was good for her pacing!" he says.

"When I was real little we had a live-in maid, and down at one end of the kitchen there was a table with an oilcloth tablecloth and a smaller table where sewing or sock darning was done. So that room had aspects of it that were like a meeting or utility space."

What has followed him through his life, however, are the old pots that came from his childhood kitchens. He still has three cast-iron skillets, a couple of inexpensive aluminum pots, and a Dutch oven pan. He remembers well when the Dutch oven pan held his mother's roast beef dinners "with the raw carrots and canned potatoes on top."

These days he is not cooking as much as he used to, and he most enjoys grilling outdoors. "When I lived in California I would cook on the grill every night; I do not put food [directly] on the grill, but food in pots and pans. There's something about that that I like a lot."

While he likes his little Connecticut cottage—"my daughters call it the bear cottage!"—it comes up a bit short on shelf space. "One of the most important things to have, which I don't [have] now is shelf space to put down the wine bottle, work with the vegetables, and plate the food. Obviously, I'd also like a gas stove. I find I don't need a large refrigerator because I would rather shop more frequently for fresh food."

Andrews' all-time favorite kitchen was the one he designed for his Santa Monica condominium with his first wife. "It was small but had enough room to move. It had red terra-cotta tiles and I installed a cooktop and a convection oven. On top of the oven I had a cutting board that must have been 3 feet by 3 feet and a half set into the countertop—made of butcher block wood—and I could lift it out of the counter and clean it at the sink."

Asked what his dream kitchen would look like, he said it would be a replica of this one. "It had a window at the sink and I could see the mountains and palm trees; there was lots of light, and a gas stovetop. I also like an oven that is capable of high temperatures. For countertops, I'd like boards that I could lift off and scrub, and mix that with Corian in a pebble gray. Style-wise, I would like it to be sleek and modern with terra-cotta tiles and lots of jars with olive oil and pasta."

OPPOSITE Take a tip from hard-working restaurants—stainless steel is the workhorse material for any kitchen, whether it is commercial or residential.

RIGHT A long country table provides a warm focal point in this sparely constructed space.

BELOW RIGHT A big wall of white tile is more likely to be found in a bathroom than a kitchen and runs the danger of looking cold and clinical—but its blank grid works well as a backdrop for a colorful display of enamel pots and pans.

FOLLOWING PAGE The modern linearity of this sophisticated cooking space doesn't detract from the living room in plain view over the bar. Sleek shapes and stainless-steel chic disguise the mess of cooking from view.

the **backsplash**

One of the most overlooked spaces in the kitchen is the backsplash because people are prone to forget about its function and think of it more as a display opportunity—the setting for decorative expression such as *elaborate* tilework or sandblasted glass. It is, nevertheless, an *essential* component of a kitchen's functionality.

The backsplash protects walls, cooktops, and sinks and should be made of material durable enough to tolerate heat and spatters. But it is also one of the most accessible spaces in the kitchen, and because of that, it has **tremendous** potential as a storage area.

Consider converting the area into a hideaway for items you use daily, particularly the bulky ones that clutter counter-tops. Open a portion of the backsplash wall to store small appliances or *accommodate* built-in shelving. Also, the backsplash itself can be outfitted with a variety of **specialty systems** to put kitchen essentials within easy reach: stainless-steel rails are one of the *handiest.* Designed to hold anything from utensils to *cups, glasses, and plates,* these can run the length of the backsplash and even come equipped with holders for a cookbook.

Hanging storage systems look best when the backsplash is simple because utensils, spice racks, or cookbooks should be considered elements of the kitchen's design—aim for visual simplicity as a crisp backdrop for your prized culinary possessions and accessories. Since today's kitchens tend to have fewer walls, take advantage of the extra space the backsplash offers: deepen the counter around the cooktop to at least 30 inches (76 cm) so that utensils can hang without getting in the way.

TIPS FOR BACKSPLASHES:

To keep the backsplash from looking cluttered—and to add to the efficiency of the work-space—remove as many of the electrical outlets as possible and run them under the cabinets. Besides being cosmetically pleasing, the bonus will be that there won't be as many expensive cut-outs in the backsplash to chop up the area.

If the counter is a slick material, such as granite or stainless steel, make the backsplash a textured material for contrast, such as slate or tumbled stone. Stay away from natural stone, however, if the counter is made from solid surfacing products such as Corian, which doesn't hold up esthetically against the material it imitates. The contrast will make the counters look cheap.

Solid-surface counters offer an opportunity to create a clean-lined profile in the kitchen and can simplify maintenance significantly. Extend the counters all the way up the wall. These integral backsplashes eliminate seams and crevices where dirt and grease collect.

ABOVE A rough-hewn central workstation and massive rock countertops mean that a serious chef doesn't have to worry about being careful—ever!

RIGHT No scrounging around in drawers is necessary when that special utensil is in plain view.

LEFT Never too much of a good thing, double refrigerators with storage drawers provide the chef with foresight enough freezer space to whip up a banquet at a moment's notice.

ABOVE Even the knives in this free-spirited cooking space are left out in the open.

CHRISTOPHER KIMBALL IS THE FOUNDER AND EDITOR OF *COOK'S ILLUSTRATED* MAGAZINE AND THE AUTHOR OF *THE COOK'S BIBLE, THE YELLOW FARMHOUSE COOKBOOK, THE BEST RECIPE, THE COOK'S ILLUSTRATED COMPLETE BOOK OF POULTRY,* AND *THE PERFECT RECIPE: GETTING IT RIGHT EVERY TIME: MAKING OUR FAVORITE DISHES THE ABSOLUTE BEST THEY CAN BE.* HE ALSO WRITES A WEEKLY COLUMN IN THE *NEW YORK DAILY NEWS.*

Christopher Kimball grew up in Westchester County, New York, and summered in Vermont. His connection to food goes way back in his life when as a young boy, he spent a lot of time at his family friend Marie Briggs' yellow farmhouse. "She was an old-time Vermonter, and town baker," he said of Briggs. "She used to cook on a green Kalamazoo stove. She'd bake thirty to forty breads and pies a day, and molasses cookies. On rainy days, or during hunting season, when I wasn't out working with the farmers, I'd sit around and watch her bake."

Her kitchen was one he remembers well. "She had a pump to the well in the sink, a little tiny pantry in the back, and another room off to the side where the cooking prep was done. She had a big Hobart to mix dough, and the main room of the house was the living room, dining room, kitchen, and a table covered with oilcloth. At lunch, there could be five or fifteen people there."

With a cow out back, there was always fresh milk to go with the warm molasses cookies, and, Kimball says, Briggs would often have a roast with potatoes cooking for dinner, and great baking powder biscuits that she'd stack for cooling.

"The floor was linoleum, and there would always be dogs on the floor. There was a big, faded green sofa, and Floyd the farmer would smoke a lot in there. The kitchen had the smell of leather, manure, baking bread, and yeast, always the smell of maple syrup, and wood from the wood stove."

Marie cooked for Norman Rockwell who later put her kitchen into the painting, *Breaking Home Ties.* This is the kitchen that has stuck in Kimball's mind his entire life. There was no kitchen at his own home that held such fertile memories. In fact, his parents "did not know much about cooking."

His kitchen in Vermont today is on his own farm, not far from the yellow farmhouse. Here, he has a few stoves including a wood-burning stove, which he enjoys. "Cooking with wood is particularly appealing...cooking is about cooking, not about food. It's about the process, and you have different woods to fiddle with."

He uses an Aga and a Viking; the Aga is used a lot for baking. The latter is not the most efficient nor easy stove to operate, but for him, that is not the priority. Besides, these stoves are, or become, members of the family.

"It's not just about organization or counter space, or the triangle, which I think is nonsense."

At the Vermont farmhouse kitchen, Kimball has a big, center counter with turned legs; he prefers, he says, to have a kitchen with furniture, not built-ins. What he does have built-in, however, are bookshelves for his cookbooks, and a pantry. "I love pantries. I make jams and jellies and honey and they're all kept in the pantry, which is dark wood. I have old yellow pine floors and brick under and behind the stoves."

"We have a trestle table, no overhanging things, and soapstone sinks. One end of the kitchen faces the valley, and we have windows that open out to the screen porch."

Room to prepare food, roll out pastry dough, or put down hot pans are essential in his kitchens. "When you're planning a kitchen, you need to think about those times you're going to have a dinner party and six pans need a place to sit!"

Also, being 6 feet, 2 inches tall, he's had his countertops made for a comfortable height to suit his frame. But, he says, even his wife, at 5 feet, 7 inches, finds the height of their counters comfortable to work at. "We've found most counters are too low, and when you're chopping vegetables, you end up with a backache."

ABOVE Well-loved and oft-used accessories are situated exactly where the cook needs them—in plain sight and close at hand.

OPPOSITE Get the most bang for the buck: if you don't have a lot of money, buy from stock and have fun creatively arranging your selections.

Put water where you need it most. Overhead faucets poised over the stovetops keep soups bubbling and save overburdened cooks the unpleasant task of toting heavy stock pots from stove to sink and back again.

kitchens as havens

FOR MANY, THE KITCHEN IS THE FAVORITE ROOM IN THE HOME.

It is the place where the meaningful transactions of the day occur—or don't occur (if you happen to think of your kitchen as a sanctuary from the hectic world). It is a microcosm of the life of the household and can resonate with your beloved objects, your signature style, and just plain quirks that make the room a pleasant hangout.

Only in the late nineteenth to early twentieth century did the kitchen become a place where the homeowner ever ventured. Formerly the domain of cooks, undercooks, and scullery maids, it wasn't even a room a householder would lay claim to, much less single out with items of personal interest. The kitchen and its noxious, lingering fumes of old cooking, were kept as far removed from notice as possible. In Victorian times, the kitchen was brought into the house, and no longer thought of in abstract terms. The British architect Robert Kerr wrote in 1864 in *The Gentleman's House* that the kitchen had acquired the character of a complicated laboratory surrounded by numerous accessories for the administration of the culinary art in all its professional details. "Laboratory" was a concept that popped up frequently during the Victorian era, probably because of a spate of inventions of gadgets and labor-saving appliances required for the four or five meals a day Victorians expected.

OPPOSITE A kitchen is the heart of the house and is often the place where families spend the most time. The unquantifiable essence of these homey kitchens is the amount of pleasure and happiness they bring to family life.

RIGHT Letting it all hang out may be just the thing for an enthusiastic cook who doesn't want to rummage through drawers for the perfect utensil.

FOLLOWING PAGE A special plate collection shouldn't be hidden away behind closed cabinet doors. Plate racks show off the design and provide safe storage too.

Today, we think of the kitchen in homier terms. While the room is first and foremost a place for cooking, it is also a place to exhibit and enjoy the things you cook with, such as cookbooks collected over the years. Cookware, china, silver, glass, and linens have also found exalted places in modern kitchens, occupying shelves and cabinets and providing a testament to the complicated and intricate associations cooking brings to a bustling daily life. The indefatigable Julia Child—chef, scholar, teacher, and collector of gadgets—stores prized pieces in her batterie de cuisine on a pegboard in her kitchen where her rolling pins and copper pans share equal ranking with paintbrushes and a transistor radio.

The secret to making the disparate elements of an idiosyncratic collection or style work in a room not traditionally disposed to personalization is consistency. If, indeed, you want to put your prized cache of plastic box purses from the fifties in your kitchen, go ahead. Just make sure that you have a lot of them to display—so it doesn't look as if a few friends with identical retro taste came to visit and left their purses behind when they went home. And display them en masse, utilizing a floor-to-ceiling shelf that a less-imaginative cook might relegate to oh-so-useful utensils or some other necessity. The collection itself becomes a design element in the room and effectively sends the message that this is a place for visual as well as gastronomic enjoyment.

RIGHT Cookbooks and favorite collections make this kitchen a place to relax and enjoy meal planning, food preparation, and dining.

RICHARD RAYMENT

EXECUTIVE CHEF RICHARD RAYMENT HAS
BEEN OVERSEEING THE FOOD AND BEVERAGE
OPERATIONS AT THE RITZ CARLTON, BOSTON
FOR THE PAST THREE YEARS. HE IS THE RECIP-
IENT OF THE GRAND CORDON D'OR DE LA
CUISINE FRANCAISE FROM THE PRINCIPALITY
OF MONACO AND WAS PRESENTED WITH THE
FIVE STAR DIAMOND AWARD, WORLD'S BEST
CHEF 1997, BY THE AMERICAN ACADEMY OF
HOSPITALITY SCIENCES.

HIS DISTINGUISHED CAREER HAS TAKEN HIM
TO LONDON'S EXCLUSIVE ST. JAMES CLUB AND
THE HAMILTON PRINCESS HOTEL IN BERMUDA,
WHERE HE WAS SELECTED TO COOK FOR HER
ROYAL HIGHNESS, PRINCESS MARGARET. A
NATIVE OF LONDON, HE GRADUATED FROM
WESTMINSTER COLLEGE. HIS PASSION FOR THE
FOOD BUSINESS GERMINATED AT THE AGE OF
FIFTEEN AT A LOCAL FISH AND CHIPS SHOP.

When Richard Rayment was growing up, his mother's kitchen was a small, modest kitchen that served a family of five boys and girls. It was always busy. "The things I remember are the equipment she had—the big mixing bowls, big hand grinder, and the scales with the heavy weights. And the view from the kitchen was amazing; it looked out to the River Thames. You could look out the window and always see something going on! I was lucky enough to eat breakfast there."

For Sunday lunches, when there would be a meal for fourteen, she often used a "hot box," which kept the vegetables warm and allowed her to prepare them ahead of time. Each vegetable had its own little compartment.

"They tell me I did have an interest in cooking, but I don't remember that until I was eleven or twelve. I do remember always licking the spoon or having the last stir!" He also enjoyed going to the food market in SoHo with his grandmother, and later, sitting and peeling potatoes with her. "SoHo had hundreds of restaurants and her apartment there was in a very old house. There wasn't even a bath."

Today, chef Rayment lives in New Hampshire and has a big kitchen that he plans to remodel. "I want to do a lot to the kitchen. Right now I look at a wall when I cook; I would like to have a freestanding area to cook from. And, I would like to make the kitchen a place where I can entertain—make it more of a gathering place."

He says cupboards are very important, and in general, he wants to have this kitchen work similarly to the way his kitchen at the Ritz does. "As a chef, you get used to having easy access to things." Likewise, he wants to use materials and create workspaces in his new kitchen that are both attractive and functional. He is considering installing granite countertops, a stainless-steel jewel sink (two in one), a cupboard for storing pots and pans, and, in general, clean lines throughout the room. "It's especially important when you want to drain off vegetables and have a place where a pot will fit," he says of the double-sink preference.

Rayment keeps his old, re-tinned, heavy copper pots for special occasions these days, and plans to get new stainless ones with a thick base. Hanging his pot collection is not in the plan; he thinks doing that just might bring the roof down!

His most cherished tools, knives, are at The Ritz, and he'll be buying new ones for his New Hampshire kitchen. "I've got hundreds of knives at The Ritz and I don't let anyone else use them! I am not a gadget person, though. I'm pretty basic. I don't need garlic presses, for example. I prefer to peel, and find it can be very therapeutic."

He plans to have all stainless-steel appliances—his stove of choice is a Viking—and a wine cabinet built for the kitchen. His biggest challenge may be to find a refrigerator that has ample storage space that also allows sensible organization. "I also hate my drawers and shelves. I like white, clean lines, and I like having light come down over the food."

ABOVE Jewel-tone coffee mugs dangle haphazardly from metal S-hooks, providing color to the plain white backdrop.

OPPOSITE Favorite pieces of art fit on a large wall and create a pleasant atmosphere for dining in the kitchen.

ABOVE A vintage metal china cabinet is just right for displaying contemporaneous pieces.

OPPOSITE Proof that task lighting doesn't always have to be serious.

kitchen **cabinets**
Cabinets have the greatest impact on how a kitchen looks. For a cook who loves to linger in the kitchen, *esthetics and function* are equally important. And, if a vital part of the kitchen's **personality** includes display of favorite items, collections, or beloved objects, cabinetry is crucial for adequate exposure as well as sensible organization. There are good ways to make storage smarter and more convenient, as well as beautiful, but knowing the choices is helpful. The main choice is whether to opt for stock or custom cabinetry.

Custom cabinetry
is a term that carries a heavy burden because it implies "expensive." The implication can be a useful one when it comes time to sell a house. But because custom cabinets are constructed to fit the space, they are often the most *practical* option in a kitchen—particularly in a kitchen renovation. Careful planning can gain inches of extra work and storage space. Sometimes, if a budget is very restricted, choosing to use custom-built cabinets can be daunting. There are, however, reasons why a serious upgrade can be a weighty factor in measuring day-to-day satisfaction, not to mention final value at resale time.

Stock cabinets, which are constructed before purchase, are like purchasing boxes that fit together. The buyer choses door style, but special sizes of units, for instance, are not available. All stock cabinets—even the fancy designer systems made with maple or cherry woods—are built to the same industry standards. Widths begin at 9 inches (22.86 cm) and increase in 3-inch (7.62 cm) increments to 48 inches (121.92 cm) (the largest size available). Often, space is left over at the end of a cabinet run, which must be covered up with a matching filler. In older homes, where the floor or the ceiling may slope just a tad, nothing short of shims and strategically placed molding will disguise the irregularity. It is a dead giveaway that the cabinets are factory built. Since some stock cabinets can be just as pricy as custom, it may be in your best interest to go with custom cabinetry.

CABINET-BUILDING MATERIALS

SINCE THE FINISH ON CABINETS HAS AN ENORMOUS IMPACT ON HOW THEY LOOK, NOT TO MENTION HOW LONG THEY LAST OR HOW EASY TO CLEAN THEY ARE, IT MAY BE ONE OF THE MOST IMPORTANT DECISIONS A HOME-OWNER CAN MAKE ABOUT THEIR KITCHEN. THREE TYPES OF CABINET FINISHES ARE DURABLE AND EASY TO CARE FOR: LAMINATE, METAL, AND THERMOPLASTIC WOOD LOOK-ALIKES. THESE CAN BE VIRTUALLY INDESTRUC-TIBLE. EVEN SO, WOOD OR WOOD VENEER ARE THE SUR-FACES OF CHOICE IN TODAY'S KITCHENS, EVEN THOUGH THEY ARE NOT AS EASY TO CLEAN.

PAINTED WOOD APPEALS TO HOMEOWNERS BECAUSE STYLE AND COLOR OPTIONS ARE SO VARIOUS. PAINTING OPENS UP COUNTLESS COLOR POSSIBILITIES, ALTHOUGH WHITE STILL REMAINS THE TOP CHOICE. STAINED WOOD CABINETS CAN WORK BEAUTIFULLY IN ROOMS THAT OPEN ONTO TRADITIONAL LIVING SPACES. THESE COMPLEMENT FURNITURE AND WOODWORK. ITS ADVANTAGE OVER PAINT IS THAT IT IS MORE DURABLE AND WON'T SHOW NICKS, SCRATCHES, OR DIRT. TO GET THE BEST OF BOTH WORLDS, USE A COLOR WASH, WHICH COMBINES THE BEST ATTRIBUTES OF PAINT AND STAIN TOGETHER. PARTICULARLY EFFECTIVE ARE INTENSE SHADES OF GREEN, BLUE, OR RED, WHICH HIGHLIGHT THE NATURAL WOOD TONES WITH SUBTLE, SEE-THROUGH COLOR. THIS EFFECT IS ESPECIALLY HARMO-NIOUS WHEN THE COLOR WASH INCORPORATES PAINT SHADES USED ELSEWHERE IN THE HOUSE. AS WITH STAINS, THE FINISHES ARE RESILIENT AND FAIRLY EASY TO CLEAN.

LEFT A formal living area blends effortlessly with the more workmanlike kitchen because the owner's taste carries through both rooms.

ABOVE An exuberant collection of colorful ceramics attests to an enthusiasm for entertaining, as well as collecting.

LYDIA SHIRE

A 1970 GRADUATE OF THE CORDON BLEU, CHEF LYDIA SHIRE HAS COOKED FOR SOME OF BOSTON'S AND CAMBRIDGE'S BEST EATERIES, INCLUDING MAISON ROBERT, THE HARVEST, THE CAFÉ PLAZA AT THE COPLEY PLAZA HOTEL, PARKER'S AT THE PARKER HOUSE, AND THE SEASONS AT THE BOSTONIAN. IN THE LATE 1980S, SHE MOVED TO THE WEST COAST TO OPEN THE FOUR SEASONS HOTEL IN BEVERLY HILLS, LANGAN'S BRASSERIE, AND THE BEVERLY RESTAURANT AND MARKET. WHEN SHE RETURNED TO BOSTON, IT WAS TO OPEN THE HIGHLY ACCLAIMED BIBA.

ydia Shire grew up in Brookline, Massachusetts, the daughter of two artists who also happened to be great cooks. Food, she says, was a "huge part of life." She remembers her dad cutting recipes out of the *New York Times*, and "making great things."

"And my mother was a great cook. The greatest thing about them was they didn't buy any junk food, as opposed to my friends' parents! And my friends used to love to comes over to eat at our house; we would eat things that were in season..."

She says the kitchen was big, and by today's standards, old-fashioned. "I can still remember when my father cooked flank steak on the pancake griddle. He'd put newspapers on the floor because it would spatter—but he knew enough to cook it hot, and technically he was a great, self-taught cook. We'd have spaghetti with olive oil, garlic, and parsley. I used to chop the garlic and parsley with a clever when I was four or five."

The kitchen had one counter and a "great big table" where all the meal prep work was done; there were lots of windows, and tall cabinets. "It was a great kitchen in its time and served its purpose well for a family with four children. We never ate in there, though; we ate all of our meals in the dining room."

Eating in the dining room is a tradition she has carried to her own home. "I think mealtime is extremely important part of the day, and I like to set a beautiful table. Even if my son Alex eats with his nanny, I insist she has candles on the table, and there is never a television on."

She, her son Alex, and husband Uriel Pineda live in a 180-year-old farmhouse in a suburb of Boston, and her kitchen has floor-to-ceiling glass windows that look out to an open field. The design is the work of her daughter, Lisa Shire, an architect. "We were her first client!"

The windows are framed in red steel, and are literally old-fashioned schoolhouse windows. Red is Shire's favorite color and it permeates this wonderful kitchen like a jumping flame. She has an old red Chambers gas stove, an Italian glass lamp over her kitchen table that looks like an octopus, and a huge 6-foot-high Italian poster with splashes of red.

The floor is concrete as is the countertop, but the latter is embedded with pieces of glass, copper, and metal, and has a tiny staircase that looks as though it was built for an ant. Little details, like rocks with wheels, a pair of glass pigs, and a silver dog, all make this a place that keeps one smiling.

"It's whimsical, and nothing in here matches. I also hate symmetry," she says pointing to the long, curved wall of glass, the four different chairs surrounding her 300-year-old Dutch tavern table made from pear wood, and the uneven breaks in her cabinetry from wood to glass.

"I have simple tools; I don't believe in a lot of gadgets, no stupid things like a júicer. And I have a big 30-gallon bucket for trash because I entertain a lot!"

The Chambers gas stove, which she loves, has a deep-fry basket, two big burners, and a little broiler oven at stovetop that allows her to brown fish topped with bread crumbs perfectly. In addition, she has a wood-burning fireplace with a rotisserie on another wall and a state-of-the-art Gaggeneau oven.

Her cabinetry is sycamore and ebony, and her pantry has a floor-to-ceiling glass window that looks out to the trees. Unlike most pantries—dark wood and shut off from the kitchen—this one is encased in see-through walls with a metallic grid sandwiched between two pieces of glass. As for paint, she says she prefers the richness and depth of oil-base paint, and is proud to say "there's not a drop of latex in here!"

She says the kitchen at Biba is as unusual as her home kitchen. "It's not that typical line of stainless-steel cooking stations. We have one, big table, and it is a visually beautiful room. People always think a restaurant kitchen has to look like a lab, but I have no white tile in here. Everything in there is strong colors, and we have an aluminum ceiling to reflect the glow of color."

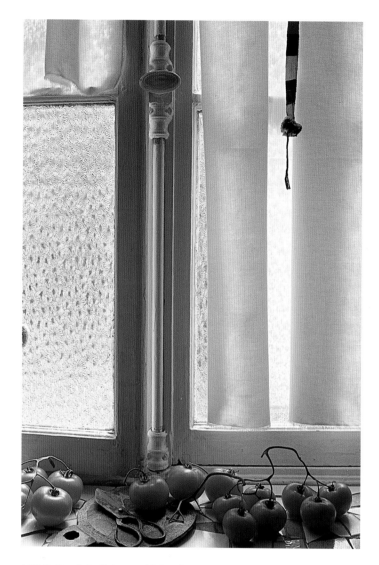

ABOVE Even just a little natural light will provide a spot for fruits and vegetables
to ripen.

OPPOSITE Strictly industrious, this kitchen gets lively invigoration from the curvy-legged
table that breaks the earnest gridwork of the backsplash and adds a touch of fun to the
room.

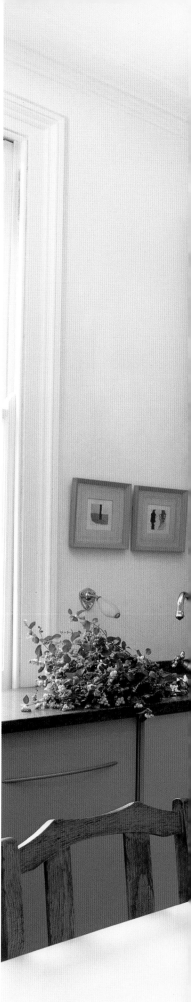

ABOVE A quirky niche provides a handy spot for a cutting board and baking supplies.

LEFT Modest materials, such as medium-density fiberboard cabinets, don't interfere with this owner's sense of style.

ABOVE An ad-hoc island with baskets casually substituting for drawers takes advantage of a wonderful sunny window—a vantage point that is good for blooming plants and ripening vegetables.

RIGHT The choice of cabinet finishes presents an important opportunity to influence the atmosphere of a cooking space. Different surface finishes, for instance, reflect the quality of light. Matte finishes, such as this subtle sage green, diffuse light and are gentle to the eye. To keep this room from being too sweet, the designer incorporated chic black countertops and a black central stove hood dramatically hanging from the ceiling.

the kitchen
as a gathering place

OF ALL THE ROOMS IN YOUR HOUSE,

THE KITCHEN IS THE MOST SOCIAL.

It is probably centrally located: there are doors to hallways, to other rooms, and to the outside. Activities are planned, carried out, and renewed in this one room—it is not just a place where the cook retreats to prepare a meal or the family assembles merely to eat. The kitchen is the heart of the home. It is a room in motion, where kids gravitate to do their homework while a parent is cooking the evening meal; it is where a television is conveniently on for Saturday-morning cartoon watching or weekday news; and it is where friends invariably congregate at parties and get-togethers—no matter how hard you try to steer them into the living or dining room.

But it wasn't always this way. In fact, only in the last decade has the kitchen evolved as the social pulse of the household. Our ancestors actually separated the kitchen from the house for safety from the hazard of fire. Later, it was separated because cooking a meal was considered a magical occurence. It was either ceremoniously toted to the dining table by staff, or the household's wife and mother, who had been at home planning and preparing the meal all day.

Today, so much has changed. Mothers usually aren't home all day and sometimes fathers are. Meal preparation is more democratic. In addition, lifestyles have become various, hectic, and complicated. The kitchen is the one place in the house where everyone can check in before dashing off to do something else and architecture has morphed to reflect the cultural shift: families want all-purpose kitchens that open to a family room, either indoors or out, or both.

OPPOSITE Pert and simple, the cooking area of this small kitchen is deftly out of sight behind a stainless-steel island.

LEFT The countertop and stovetop form a continuous line—a good design decision in this small kitchen because it adds continuity as well as good looks.

Here, activities can remain focused—at least for a while—and a parent can keep an eye on the comings and goings of children, guests, pets, and friends.

And when it comes time to throw a party, host and hostess can fix a meal and still mingle with guests. It might even be good for the hostess—and her guests: In 1898, economist-feminist Charlotte Perkins Gilmore argued for cooperative kitchens in her treatise "Women and Economics" on the grounds that such an arrangement would improve life and love for both men and women, married or single.

The big challenge for designing a kitchen that is a gathering space is to remember that since this is a place that will be the center of family life, it should be arranged with distinct zones in mind. Ideally, the cooking area (preferably an island) will face into the room and function as a kind of command central; there should be an informal eating area; and a relaxation area, with sofa, chairs, and play area, should be beyond. A desk with space for personal computer for household administration, homework, and game playing might occupy a nearby niche.

Although modern life is wildly different from anything our parents could have envisioned, one thing remains the same. Think back to your childhood and you will probably recall vivid memories of dinnertime with your family because so much family drama occurred there. It still does today. For this reason alone, a kitchen as a gathering space will always be more than just a place for cooking. It is a welcoming space where everyone migrates, for company and for food.

FOR KIDS ONLY

SINCE THE KITCHEN IS AN ALL-PURPOSE SPACE, BRING ORDER TO THE INEVITABLE CHAOS BY INCLUDING IN YOUR PLANS A PULL-OUT DRAWER WHERE TOYS CAN BE QUICKLY STOWED. IF YOU HAVE A WINDOW IN THE ROOM, INSTALLING A WINDOW SEAT COULD BE THE ANSWER TO A STORAGE SHORTAGE.

A CENTRAL COOKING ISLAND IS A GOOD PLACE TO INCLUDE A CHILD-HEIGHT COUNTER FOR THE YOUNGER MEMBERS OF YOUR FAMILY. RUN A LOW SHELF ACROSS A LENGTH OF THE ISLAND FOR A GOOD SPOT FOR KIDS TO PURSUE THEIR OWN COOKING INTERESTS OR ENJOY MEALS IN A SPACE OF THEIR OWN. DURING BUSY MEAL PREPARATION, THE LOW COUNTER IS A CONVENIENT AREA TO USE ELECTRICAL APPLIANCES.

NICK STELLINO

NICK STELLINO'S FIRST JOB IN A RESTAURANT CAME IN HIS MID-THIRTIES AS A DISHWASH-ER. HIS DREAM TO BECOME A CHEF AND OWN HIS OWN RESTAURANT WOULD COME IN JUST ONE YEAR. FROM THERE, HIS COOKING CAREER CAUGHT ON FIRE. HE QUICKLY WENT FROM BEING A CHEF TO CREATING A TELEVISION SERIES ABOUT ITALIAN COOKING, AND WRIT-ING A COMPANION COOKBOOK. *CUCINA AMORE* AIRED ON PBS FOR THE FIRST TIME IN 1995, AND HE PROCEEDED TO FILM 143 MORE EPISODES.

TODAY, HE IS THE AUTHOR OF FOUR COOK-BOOKS: *CUCINA AMORE, GLORIOUS ITALIAN COOKING, MEDITERRANEAN FLAVORS,* AND *NICK STELLINO'S FAMILY KITCHEN.* THE POPU-LAR PBS DOCUMENTARY, *ITALIAN-AMERICAN II,* WITH STELLINO AS THE STAR, WON AN EMMY. THE *NEW YORK TIMES* SELECTED STELLINO TO AUTHOR THE ITALIAN FOOD AND WINE SUPPLEMENT FOR THEIR WEEKEND MAGAZINE. IN ADDITION, HE IS A FAMILIAR FACE ON THE *TODAY SHOW, OPRAH,* AND *GOOD MORNING AMERICA.*

Nick Stellino was born and raised in Palermo, Sicily, and meal time and the kitchen were the focal points of the day. "In the morning, we ate breakfast together, and the first question asked was what's for dinner? And we'd ask my mother 'How are you going to make it?' I'd ask, 'Are you going to put the spices under the skin?' And I'd ask 'How are you going to do the potatoes?'"

The kitchen, where his mother prepared meals for Nick, his brother Mario, and his father, was modest and was in the middle of a working-class neigh-borhood. It was his mother's unique cooking that distinguished the smells coming out of her kitchen from others. "What she did was different from the lady next door."

"Our kitchen was small, with a very small gas stove. There was a family table in the middle of the room, and no luxuries except for the refrigerator my mother got for her tenth anniversary. She was very excited about that."

The view was of other buildings in the front and back of this five-story building and Nick remembers how he could see into other family's kitchens. "My mother would hang her clothes out there, and in the morning she would talk to the senora across the way. There was a sense of tightness in the neighborhood and the world revolved around that kitchen. It was the heart of the house."

For Nick, the kitchen held within its walls the voices of his life; if they could speak, they would tell the story of this loving family. It was in this kitchen that Nick asked his father's permission to come to America. It is where he told his father of his first broken heart, where he first saw his parents dancing, where there were emotional family squabbles and where peace came swiftly. "And it was just an average, unpretentious room. You don't need a Viking stove to make a kitchen. This was painted in a glaze of love, a magical room."

Nick also spent time in the kitchen of his maternal grandmother, Adele. "She was really responsible for getting me started. She taught me how to cook; she taught me about onions, and to this day when I cook them I feel she's with me. I used to love to stir them and watch them turn translucent." Her kitchen, living room, and family room were one, and it had an open hearth to cook on. "She was truly poor... the most unpretentious woman I ever met, and she made a ragout and gnocchi that was unbelievable."

Today, Nick's kitchen is also modest and small. It has a tiny table for two, and he describes it as looking like the galley in a boat. "I have the best of equipment, but no space. And that trains me to be organized. It's ten steps in one direction and five in the other, and it's painted red—my favorite color."

He has not had a dishwasher in twenty years, "and that accounts for my formed biceps and forearm! There are no countertops; I basically have a 3 foot by 3 foot area."

Asked if he has favorite pots and pans, or certain must-have gadgets, he is quick to say, "I fall in love with nothing except for my father's watch. There is nothing in there that I cannot do without. And if I don't have what I need to do something, I make it happen with whatever is available; I've done that cooking for thirty or three hundred people."

The most important thing to Nick is the people in the kitchen and the food you share. "A dinner table today is the last place where we meet as a tribe—that goes back to the caveman days. And I think that the family that eats together stays together."

OPPOSITE Paint color and pale woods in furniture and woodwork are coordinated between living room and kitchen so that the transition between the two rooms appears effortless.

ABOVE Angled toward a corner of the kitchen, this wedge-shaped island expresses a dynamic principle and suggests that this is where all the action is.

ABOVE Obviously a place to have fun, this merry kitchen comes equipped with its own jukebox.

RIGHT This kitchen doesn't take itself too seriously—a checkerboard of green-and-white tiles forms the backsplash while other colors find liberal expression elsewhere.

flooring

The kitchen is the center of *activity* in the home and, therefore, it experiences a lot of wear and tear—especially the floor. Plan accordingly, but don't assume that the most durable floor (concrete, for instance) is the best choice. Options range from soft (such as woods and vinyls) to harder (such as slate and limestone tiles) to hardest (concrete and ceramics), but there are **other considerations.** Aesthetics, hygeine, durability, and cost must all be considered before choosing a flooring material.

Wood. For warmth of tone and forgiveness underfoot, natural or recycled wood is a kitchen favorite. It is easy to keep clean, but requires extra protection around wet areas such as the sink. Also, in a kitchen that already has wood cabinetry and counters, wood on the floor may be too much of a good thing.

Vinyl. Vinyl is a manmade plastic and comes in a wide array of colors and patterns. It is soft underfoot (and will ripple if your floor is uneven) and absorbs sound, but tends to discolor with age. Some vinyls require waxing, which can be an annoying and recurrent maintenance obligation.

Linoleum. Made from natural materials such as linseed oil, linoleum is similar to vinyl in that it comes in a wide variety of colors and patterns. Also soft underfoot and sound-absorbent, it is durable and generally low maintenance (requires some polishing to counteract scuffing). It comes in sheets or squares—but unsealed seams can become conduits for water seepage.

Slate and limestone. The appeal of these softer stones (as opposed to granite and marble) is that they have rock-solid staying power and, if properly sealed, will wear well over the years. Colors are alluring, too. Slates range from gray to green to purple; limestone tends toward neutral tones. But, don't forget that they are rock—these materials will be cold underfoot and reflect noise. Lighter colors also show dirt easily.

Ceramics and concrete. The most durable of flooring materials, ceramics and concrete are virtually indestructible. However, their durability is also their main drawback: the materials can be hard on the feet and legs, brutal to dropped dishes, and slippery when wet.

PREVIOUS PAGE With a wall of windows open to the outdoors, the black metal bistro chairs are a happy accessory to casual dining.

LEFT Time has stopped in this all-purpose kitchen where cooking, eating, and even clothes washing and drying coexist in fresh and colorful harmony.

GILES THOMPSON

A MEMBER OF THE ACADEMY OF CULINARY
ARTS, EXECUTIVE CHEF GILES THOMPSON IS
RESPONSIBLE FOR ALL MENUS AT THE RITZ
RESTAURANT, THE PALM COURT, PRIVATE DIN-
ING ROOMS, AND ROOM SERVICE. PRIOR TO
JOINING THE RITZ, LONDON, HE WORKED FOR
NINE YEARS, PERFECTING HIS COOKING
SKILLS AT THE CONNAUGHT UNDER THE DIREC-
TION OF EXECUTIVE CHEF MICHAEL BOURDIN.
HE WAS REWARDED IN 1996 WHEN HE MOVED
TO DANESFIELD HOUSE, BUCKINGHAMSHIRE,
WHERE HE QUICKLY ACHIEVED TWO AA
ROSETTES AND AN RAC RESTAURANT AWARD.

Giles Thompson was born in Halifax and comes from a family of butchers. When he was only eight or nine, he would ride in his father's van and accompany him to the schools to make food deliveries. "I'd be greeted by big matron-type ladies who spoiled me with pastries and other beautiful foods."

The other food influence in his life was his mother. "My mother was a very keen home cook and, in the traditional sense, a housewife. The main part of her day was spent preparing food and cooking. She looked after the appetites of the family.

"We lived in an old Victorian house, and the kitchen had a country feel to it, but it was very much a working kitchen. I remember a big wooden table in the kitchen, and the Aga stove that was cream colored. The cellar had a food storage area and there were stone salting blocks."

"In my ideal kitchen, I would very much like to take on a lot of those ideas and that sentiment."

He and his wife live in a cozy, converted old stable in a neighborhood with cobblestone streets, fronted by grand houses with their stables converted to homes. Once the sleeping quarters for grooms, the space is quite restricted, and the kitchen here is a little galley. "I like the galley kitchen because for one person working in here it has everything at hand, close by, and you can concentrate."

He's quite used to cooking in confined quarters since he spent many days as a young man, just out of college cooking on boats. "On the boats, I used to prepare twenty to thirty gourmet meals a day."

He has easy-to-care-for granite countertops and a wooden floor, which he says maintains the charming cottage feel. The most important ingredients here, though, are his cherished tools— a small chopping block complete with slots for his knives and an iron rail overhead for all of his utensils and gadgets. "I buy lots of gadgets—graters, peelers, crushers. And I treasure my Moulenex blender!" He looks forward to the summer view out his window when his window boxes will be brimming with colorful geraniums.

Thompson cooks off an Electrolux ceramic-topped stove, which he inherited with the space— perfect, he says for home cooking. The ceramic top gives off a good amount of heat; almost like a gas stove would.

All of this is in sharp contrast to his kitchen at The Ritz where he spends lots of his time moving about a large kitchen. Following a recent refurbishment program, a windowed office was built for him in the center of the kitchen. From there he can sit and watch the progress of room service, prep, and the patisserie.

"Here, there is a much better layout." And, here is where his prized, custom-built French Rouge stove will soon sit. He describes this as a very traditional stove that at 50,000 to 60,000 pounds, will also be a conversation piece in his kitchen.

"At my dream house, there will be children crawling around my feet, and they'll pick up the trade and complete the circle! I can see that new kitchen coming."

Tucked into the corner of this great room with soaring cathedral ceilings, the kitchen is command central for large gatherings.

LEFT A bare suggestion of the outdoors outside the kitchen's glass doors turns into a riotous invasion of tropical plants and water in the dining area—a surprise against the clean lines and pristine colors of modern design.

ABOVE Cool, calm, and collected, this kitchen is a place to get away from it all—the soft translucence of the cabinets and the pristine color suggest that this is a world away from the rat race.

kitchen traditions

NOW THAT THEY DON'T HAVE TO DO THE DIRTY WORK ANY MORE,

COOKS CAN INDULGE IN LITTLE
APPLIANCES THAT ARE FOR FUN ONLY,

like crepe makers, pasta makers, and choppers that julienne vegetables precisely and elaborately. Since refrigerators self-defrost, stoves self-clean, and dishwashers abolish even the densest scum from pans, cooks can dedicate areas in their kitchens—or outside, for that matter—to the pursuit of these finer pleasures. Baking alcoves, open-air kitchens, wine-tasting nooks, and other rebuttals of the standardized kitchen are all a result of our love of personalization and of the availability of professional-grade appliances that allow even the amateur to pursue and enjoy a singular gastronomic passion.

Civilized people have always been creative about finding places to cook a meal—and have never been deterred by unfavorable circumstances, such as the nonexistence of a formal kitchen. Campfire cooking, an unglamorous necessity of the pioneering life, remains with us in our backyard barbecues. In the mid-twentieth century, outdoor cooking swerved perilously close to becoming the cliche of American suburban life—the only way some adults now remember their parents (usually fathers) had to commune with nature. The actual meal might even have been anticlimactic.

Nowadays such exotic variations on predictable culinary pursuits evolve more out of a homeowner's curiosity rather than necessity. There are so many options besides cooking that can take place in a kitchen—and so many gadgets and appliances with which to pursue those options. Ironically, with a plug-in gadget for nearly every task imaginable, our lives in the kitchen have not necessarily become easier. The proliferation of gadgets was originally billed as the way to lessen the burdens of our home life. "Living Better—Electrically" was GE's succinct promise. One thing the plethora of gadgets has provided, though, is a way for us to be more creative. For imaginative cooks, the only thing missing in a perfect kitchen is a special place to pursue a beloved pastime, such as grilling or wine tasting.

OPPOSITE Dream kitchens come in all shapes and sizes. The best cooking spaces make the best of all available space.

FOLLOWING PAGE A pink gingham tablecloth adds curious civility to this rustic kitchen with stone walls. The long wood table and hodgepodge of chairs are an open invitation to join in the fun.

Finding a location amenable to a cooking hobby can be easy—a neglected closet or space under a stair offers ample storage for wine. The enterprising baker can transform an outdated breakfast nook into a utilitarian baking alcove. Or, move out of the kitchen entirely and set up an oven and grill outside—an effortless solution to too much heat in the kitchen. These kitchens-within-a-kitchen are the one aspect of kitchen design where rules don't have to prevail. They are the ultimate indulgence and usually occupy a place of honor in, or near, the kitchen. Perhaps the ideal arrangement is one in which the cook can be both at work and at play at the same time—with the favorite nook close enough to the rest of the appliances to keep a sense of continuity going when food preparation is in full swing, but also far enough away to provide a sense of freedom from the obligations meal preparation often implies.

ABOVE Personalizing a kitchen can be as simple as selecting cookware in a distinctive color. The visual impact of color and shape is an effective design tool.

OPPOSITE A modern rustic kitchen evokes warmth; the central island—topped with durable stainless steel—is generously sized for friends and family to gather around.

CORBY KUMMER

CORBY KUMMER'S WORK FOR THE *ATLANTIC MONTHLY* HAS ESTABLISHED HIM AS ONE OF THE MOST WIDELY READ, AUTHORITATIVE, AND CREATIVE FOOD WRITERS IN THE UNITED STATES. THE *SAN FRANCISCO EXAMINER* PRONOUNCES HIM "A DEAN AMONG FOOD WRITERS IN AMERICA." KUMMER'S RECENT BOOK, *THE JOY OF COFFEE*, HAS ALREADY BEEN HERALDED BY THE *NEW YORK TIMES* AS "THE MOST DEFINITIVE AND ENGAGINGLY WRITTEN BOOK ON THE SUBJECT TO DATE."

GIORGIO DELUCA, COFOUNDER OF NEW YORK'S EPICUREAN GROCERY DEAN & DELUCA, SAYS: "I CAN TELL WHEN CORBY'S PIECES HIT; THE PHONE DOESN'T STOP RINGING." IN NOMINATING HIS WORK FOR A NATIONAL MAGAZINE AWARD (AND FOR WHICH HE BECAME A FINALIST), THE EDITORS WROTE: "KUMMER TREATS FOOD AS IF ITS PREPARATION WERE SOMETHING OF A LIFE SPORT: AN ACTIVITY TO BE PURSUED REGULARLY AND HEALTHFULLY BY KNOWLEDGEABLE PEOPLE WHO DEMAND QUALITY." THE YALE GRADUATE IS ALSO A FREQUENT FOOD COMMENTATOR ON TELEVISION AND RADIO.

Corby Kummer grew up in Connecticut and has fond memories of his mother cooking breakfast while she chatted with him. The kitchen, he says, was "a late-1950s St. Charles-styled room with metal cabinets and nifty built-in features."

"What I loved was seeing the breakfast table from the counter-high stove and cutting board; there were built-in cutting boards. She could cook and talk to us if we were sitting down. I really like the mingling of cooking and dining."

Today, Kummer lives on Boston's Beacon Hill and his kitchen overlooks Charles Street, a narrow, charming street filled with antique and specialty shops, and cafes. "I have a big butcher block table that looks out to the street and I watch people shopping. ... I delight in that. I also have a dining room table in my living room, so if my stove and sink are dirty, people at the dining room table can't see it. And if I'm at the chopping block, I can still talk to people." Kummer says he finds the best conversation comes while he is preparing a meal for his guests—just like when he used to talk to his mother as she cooked his dinner.

Being in a rental, he has not done any major construction to create a Kummer kitchen. What he has added has been practical. "I did install a counter with shelves. I'd love to have cabinets that closed. But here, everything is out. I've got a pegboard and very little is in drawers or behind doors."

The plus of having all his tools on the pegboard or shelves is that they're easily accessible. He also uses magnetic racks for tools, a shelf for frequently used ingredients, a cutting board (nearby!), and metro shelving with bowls at his chest and shoulder height.

Closed cabinets would be good, he says, for tools less frequently used. "I don't dream of a large kitchen. All I would like is more storage." Specifically, he would like a cold-storage pantry for his canned vegetables, polenta, whole wheat flower, and olive oil. A cool, dark place is perfect for those ingredients.

"If someone has a basement, I envy them! I'm longing for that. I've spent a lot of time in Italian homes and kitchens and they have lots of cold storage."

His palette of choice is beige and egg yolk yellow for a kitchen. "I don't like seeing bright colors when I'm thinking about food, or putting it together. I like to think about the colors of the food, which all change by the season; that is what should determine what you put on plates."

As for pots, pans, and gadgets, he says he really only needs his Alessi pasta pot with the perforated insert that "heats beautifully, and looks like a piece of sculpture," a good sauce pan, saute pan, and a kettle.

"Like many beginning cooks I spent all of my earnings on fancy equipment, and with the exception of a mandolin and beautiful Kitchen Aid, the rest I should give away... I think there is an idea out there that equipment makes a better cook but the best cooks I've met, the legendary grandmothers, are using old pans, and the cheapest pans!"

LEFT For breakable collections, high shelving offers safe display and clever use of often-wasted space.

ABOVE Is it blue and white or glass that the owner obviously loves? Either way, both passions can be expressed in this happy arrangement of tile backsplash and open shelving where little blue and white glasses are neatly arrayed.

A glowing fire reminds diners in this rustic-beamed kitchen that hospitality and companionship are the main reason friends like to eat together.

ventilation

ventilation If there is one thing that distinguishes the modern kitchen from its *old-fashioned* counterpart, it's ventilation. Stale cooking odors lingering in a house used to be the hallmark of bad housekeeping. Opening a window and hoping a *sudden breeze* would eliminate the problem was not a good solution. Nowadays, ventilation systems are so thorough—if not voracious—in consuming fumes as well as steam and even gas, that kitchens not only seem cleaner, they are cleaner.

Kitchen ventilation systems fall into two categories: **updraft and downdraft.** Updraft ventilation comes with a blower and a hood and captures cooking grease and fumes as it billows off the stove and vents them right out of the house. Commercial cooking appliances usually require updraft ventilation systems.

Downdraft ventilation systems are not as effective, but have the advantage of being less obtrusive (not always a bonus since smart kitchen designers make the stove hood a major focal element). By producing an area of low pressure just above burner lever to draw hot air and fumes down and out of the house, downdraft ventilation systems are often used in island cooktops where there is no option for a stove hood. Just remember to get a fan powerful enough to remove fumes without making the kitchen so noisy guests must shout over the roar. One standard of measurement is the size of the stovetop—the larger this is, the larger the fan needs to be. Exhaust is measured in cubic feet per minute (cfm). A fan rated 350 cfm is adequate for residential use; commercial-style ranges may require up to 1200 cfm. Keep things quiet with a low sones measurement—typical kitchen exhaust fans range from 4.5 to 7 sones.

ABOVE No wasted space here, as an inventive designer has taken advantage of often-overlooked blank space and turned the door fronts of storage cabinets into blackboards for notes and menus.

RIGHT Kitchens are intensely personal spaces—the best of them have the mark of their owner indelibly expressed within.

Outdoor kitchens are the ultimate in no-muss, no-fuss philosophy. In warm climates, this kind of culinary abandon makes perfect sense.

THE MODERN KITCHEN

THE NEW, MODERN KITCHEN HAS BEEN FREED FROM ITS OLD CONFINES—IN MATERIALS, IN FLOOR PLAN, IN NEW EFFICIENCIES, AND IN EXPECTATIONS. SOME OF THE NEWEST KITCHENS ARE SO STRIPPED DOWN, THAT THEIR BASIC SIMPLICITY IS THE GREATEST FREEDOM OF ALL. OTHERS HAVE ALL THE GADGETS. THESE GADGETS ARE THE ANSWER TO TODAY'S DILEMMAS OF LACK OF SPACE AND LACK OF TIME, AND A MODERN WISHLIST WOULD HAVE AT LEAST SOME OF THESE FOR THE PERFECT KITCHEN:

- NEW, FOUR-COMPARTMENT, ANODIZED ALUMINUM GARBAGE CANS ON WHEELS CAN GO EVERYWHERE WITH THE COOK. TWO SIZES OF PLASTIC INSERTS ON TOP AND A DRAWER ON THE BOTTOM SEPARATE RECYCLABLES AND WASTE FOR EASY DISPOSAL.

- AWKWARD CABINETS IN NARROW SPACES BECOME USEABLE WHEN THEY ARE OUTFITTED WITH PULLOUT SHELVES TO HOLD SPICES AND CONDIMENTS.

- SLIDES, SHELVES, HOOKS, AND SEALED MINICABINETS MAKE PANTRY SYSTEMS RECONFIGURABLE AND ADAPTABLE TO THE KIND OF FOOD STORAGE A COOK REALLY NEEDS.

- THE KICK PLATE UNDER THE CABINET DOESN'T HAVE TO BE WASTED SPACE. HERE, DRAWERS CAN BE ADDED TO HOLD STEPLADDERS, ACCESSORIES, AND KITCHEN HARDWARE.

- RESTAURANT-STYLE TRAYS OUTFITTED WITH CANISTERS KEEP BEANS, RICE, FLOUR, AND SUGAR DRY AND NEAT. THEY CAN BE INSTALLED IN A DRAWER AND FREE THE COUNTER OF CLUTTER, NOT TO MENTION INEVITABLE SPILLAGE.

- UTENSIL DRAWERS NOW COME WITH CUTOUTS FOR STANDARD KITCHEN TOOLS, INCLUDING CORKSCREWS AND ZESTERS.

- POT AND PAN LIDS CAN BE ONE OF THE KITCHEN'S GREATEST ANNOYANCES. NEW DRAWERS WITH WOODEN SLATS KEEP TOPS FROM GOING AWRY.

RUTH ROGERS

KNOWN FOR HER EXQUISITE COOKING AT THE RIVER CAFÉ, LONDON, AND THEIR COOKBOOKS, RUTH ROGERS, ALONG WITH HER CHEF PARTNER ROSE GRAY, SEEM TO CONTINUOUSLY CAPTURE KUDOS IN THE KITCHEN. THEIR BOOK, *THE RIVER CAFÉ COOKBOOK* IS THE WINNER OF THE GLENFIDDICH FOOD BOOK OF THE YEAR AND THE BCA ILLUSTRATED BOOK OF THE YEAR AWARDS. THE COOKING DUO HAVE ALSO AUTHORED *THE RIVER CAFÉ BOOK TWO* AND *RIVER CAFÉ ITALIAN KITCHEN,* WHICH HAVE ALSO GOTTEN RAVE REVIEWS.

Ruth Rogers spent her childhood in the Catskill Mountains, in the little town of Woodstock. With three siblings, and parents who came from very large families, she recalls "many, many large family meals."

"A lot of our life revolved around the kitchen table. My father's mother was an amazing cook and when she visited, she spent all of her time in the kitchen...food, eating, and talking was a big part of our lives."

Two moves within Woodstock and the two family kitchens designed by her parents shared a common thread: "there was a lot of space, and the main living area was one big room that included the kitchen, dining room, and living room. There was always a window looking out to the countryside, and a sense that this was a place where everyone was welcome and enjoyed being. That's where you came... to the kitchen!"

Interestingly, she says, her parents planned those big, open rooms to purposefully keep everyone together. "There were large work areas, places for people to sit and eat, stools where people could sit and watch you cook. They were big houses, and entering the house smelling cooking smells was always a part of my life." Ironically, she says her husband, an architect, has designed all of his kitchens without walls separating them from the main living space as well.

The couple's home today continues the tradition, allowing family members to work and be together in the kitchen. But, unlike her mother who kept things like pots, pans, and kitchen tools out in the open, Ruth prefers a cleaner, more minimalist look. "Today, I live in London, overlooking a park. We bought two houses and put them together. The house has one big, main living space, and the kitchen area has a big stainless-steel island that serves as my platform. Everything is put away; you see two sinks, and that's it."

Countertops are stainless, and the kitchen is equipped with Gaggeneau ovens and a gas stovetop. She grills on the terrace barbecue.

Rogers says The River Café's kitchen is exposed to the restaurant patrons, has lots of stainless steel, and all the workspaces have big windows overlooking the river and garden. "It's not a large kitchen; we keep it domestic in scale, and it's a nice place to work. The person who cleans the pots and pans, who often works without a view, has a view of the river here!"

ABOVE A rustic island is the focal point in this cooking space tucked neatly under a sleeping space.

RIGHT A wood-fired baking oven may be harder to use than a conventional stove, but bread cooked in it will definitely taste better.

Some cooks are sentimental—perhaps even superstitious—about what they cook on. An ancient black stove has produced generations of meals and food cooked on it now is probably all the better for it.

RESOURCE LIST

ACCESSORIES

ABC Carpet and Home
881 & 888 Broadway at
E. 19th Street
New York, NY 10003
(212)473-3000
www.abchome.com

Aero Furniture
011-44-181-971-0022

Alchemy
(310)836-8631
www.alchemy-glass.com

Anthropologie
1700 Sansom Street, 6th Floor
Philadelphia, PA 19103
1-800-309-2500/ 1-800-543-1039
www.anthropologie.com

Bed, Bath and Beyond
1-800-GO-BEYOND
www.bedbathandbeyond.com

The Bombay Company
P.O. Box 161009
Fort Worth, TX 76161-1009
1-800-829-7789
www.bombayco.com

Cappellini-Modern Age
102 Wooster Street
New York, NY 10012
(212)966-0669
www.cappelini.it

The Conran Shop
Michelin House
81 Fulham Road
London SW3 6RD
0171-591-8702
www.conran.co.uk

The Container Store
200 Valwood Parkway
Dallas, TX 75234-8800
1-800-733-3532
www.containerstore.com

Crate & Barrel
www.crateandbarrel.com

Dean and Deluca
2526 East 36th St. North Circle
Wichita, Kansas 67219
1-800-781-4050
www.deandeluca.com

Essential Home
3775 24th Street
San Francisco, CA 94114
1-888-282-3330
www.essentialhome.com

Gardener's Eden
P.O. Box 7307
San Francisco, CA 94120-7307
1-800-822-9600

Garnet Hill
1-800-622-6216
www.garnethill.com

IKEA
1-800-434-ikea
www.ikea.com

Kitchen Etc...
32 Industrial Drive
Exeter, NH 03833
1-800-232-4070
www.kitchenetc.com

Kmart
1-800-63-KMART
www.bluelight.com

Linens 'n Things
6 Brighton Road
Clifton, NJ 07015
(973)815-2974
www.linensnthings.com

Pier 1 Imports
461 Fifth Avenue
New York, NY 10017
1-800-447-4371
www.pier1.com

Placewares
160 Newbury Street
Boston, MA 02116-2833
(617)267-5460
www.placewares.com

Pottery Barn
P.O.Box 7044
San Francisco, CA 94120
1-800-922-5507
www.potterybarn.com

Smith + Hawken
1-800-940-1170
www.smithandhawken.com

Spiegel
P.O.Box 182555
Columbus, OH 43218-2555
1-800-474-5555
www.spiegel.com

Takashimaya
693 Fifth Avenue
New York, NY 10022
1-800-753-2038

Target
1-888-304-4000
www.target.com

Urban Archaeology
143 Franklin Street
New York, NY 10013
(212)431-4646

Urban Outfitters
4040 Locust Street
Philadelphia, PA 19104
(215)387-0373

Williams-Sonoma
1-800-840-2591
www.williams-sonoma.com

CABINETS

Adelphi Custom Cabinetry
Box 1267
Robesonia, PA 19551
1-800-992-3101

Aristokraft
(812)482-2527
www.aristocraft.com

The Conran Shop
Michelin House
81 Fulham Road
London SW3 6RD
0171-591-8702
www.conran.co.uk

The Container Store
200 Valwood Parkway
Dallas, TX 75234-8800
1-800-733-3532

Crate and Barrel
www.crateandbarrel.com

Decora
(812)2634-2288
www.decoracabinets.com

Fieldstone
1-800-339-5369
www.fieldstonecabinetry.com

Heritage
(717)354-4011
www.hck.com

IKEA
1-800-434-ikea
www.ikea.com

Johnny Grey and Co. USA
49 Rt 202
Far Hills, NJ 07931
(908)781-1554

Kraftmaid
1-800-571-1 990
www.kraftmaid.com

Merillat/Amera
1-800-575-8763 or
(517)263-0771 (Amera)
www.merillat.com

Omega
(319)236-2256
www.omegacab.com

Plain & Fancy
1-800-420-7888
www.homeportfolio.com

Renovator's Supply
Box 2525
Conway, NH 94120
1-800-922-5507

Rutt
1-800-420-7888
www.ruttl.com

Siematic
1-800-765-5266
www.siematic.com

Snaidero
201 West 132nd Street
Los Angeles, CA 90061
(310)516-8499

Wellborn
1-800-336-8040
www.wellborncabinet.com

Wood-mode
1-800-635-7500
www.wood-mode.com

Yorktowne
1-800-777-0065
www.yorktowneinc.com

FLOORING

American Olean Tile Co.
1000 Cannon Avenue
Lansdale, PA 19446
(215)855-1111

Armstrong World Industries
Adistra Corp
101 Union Street
Plymouth, MI 48170
1-800-714-8000

Congoleum, Princeton Pike
Corporate Center #1
989 Lenos Drive
Lawrenceville, NH 08648
1-800-934-3567

Country Floors
15 East 16th Street
NY, NY 10003
(212)627-8300

Mannington Wood Floors
Mannington Mills
1327 Lincon Drive
High Pond, NC 27260
1-800-252-4202

Ann Sacks Tile and Stone
8120 NE 33rd
Portland, OR 97211
(503)281-7751

Tarkett
800 Lanidex Plaza
Parsippany, NJ 07054
1-800-827-5388

MAJOR APPLIANCE MANUFACTURERS

Amana
2800 220th Trail.
Box 8901
Aman, IA 52204-0001
1-800-843-0304
www.amana.com

EBA Wholesale
2361 Nostrand Avenue
Brooklyn, NY 11210
1-800-380-2378

Frigidaire Co.
Box 7181
Dublin, OH 43017
1-800-685-6005
www.frigidaire.com

Gaggenau USA
425 University Avenue
Norwood, MA 020062
(617)255-1766

GE Appliances
Appliance Park
Louisville, KY 40225
1-800-626-2000
www.generalelectric.com

Jenn-Air
240 Edwards St SE
Cleveland, TN 37311
1-800-536-6247
www.jennair.com

KitchenAid
2000 M-63
MailDrop 4302
Benton Harbor, MI 49022
1-800-253-3977
www.kitchenaid.com

LVT Price Quote Hotline
(516)234-8884
email: callvt@aol.com

Maytag Co.
403 West 4th St North
Newton, IA 50208
1-800-688-9900
www.maytag.com

Sub-Zero Freezer Co.
Box 44130
Madison, WE 53744
1-800-444-7820
www.subzero.com

Tappan Appliances
6000 Perimeter Circle
Dublin, OH 43017
1-800-685-6005
www.tappan.com

Thermador
Masco Corp.
5119 District Blvd
Los Angeles, CA 90040
(213)562-1133
www.thermador.com

Viking Range Corp
111 Front Street
Greenwood, MS 38930
(601)455-1200
www.vikingrange.com

Whirlpool Corp
2000 M-63
Mail Drop 4303
Benton Harbor, MI 49022
1-800-253-1301
www.whirlpool.com

Westinghouse/Frigidaire
600 Perimeter Drive
Dublin, OH 43017
1-800-374-4434
www.westinghouse.com

LIGHTING

Elkay Manufacturing Co
2222 Camden Court
Oak Brook, IL 60521
(630)574-8484
www.elkay.com

Golden Valley Lighting
274 Eastchester Drive
High Point, NC 27262
1-800-735-3377

Lightolier
631 Airport Road
Fall River, MA 02720
(508)679-8131
www.lightolier.com

Lightning Bug
320 W 202 Street
Chicago Heights, IL 60411
1-800-323-3226

Luminaire
301 West Superior
Chicago, IL 60610
1-800-494-4358

Ovation
73 Lafayette Street
Marblehead, MA 01945
(781)639-4754
www.ovationfurniture.com

Poulsen Lighting
3260 Meridian Parkway
Fort Lauderdale, FL 33331
(954)349-2525

Task Lighting Corporation
Box 1090
910 East 25th
Kearney, NY 68848
1-800-445-6404

HARDWARE
American Standard
Box 6820
One Centennial Plaza
Piscataway, NY 08855
1-800-7 52-6292
www.americanstandard.com

The Conran Shop
Michelin House
81 Fulham Road
London SW3 6RD
0171-591-8702
www.conran.co.uk

Crate & Barrel
www.crateandbarrel.com

Essential Home
3775 24th Street
San Francisco, CA 94114
1-888-282-3330
www.essentialhome.com

Delta Faucet
Masco Corp
55 E. 111 Street
Indianapolis, IN 46280
(317)848-1812
www.deltafaucet.com

Eljer Plumbingware
17120 Dallas Parkway
Dallas, TX 75248
(972)402-2600
www.eljer.com

Franke Kitchen Systems
212 Church Road
North Wales, PA 19454
1-800-626-5771

IKEA
1-800-434-ikea
www.ikea.com

Kitchen Etc...
32 Industrial Drive
Exeter, NH 03833
1-800-232-4070
www.kitchenetc.com

Kohler Co.
444 Highland Drive
Kohler, WI 53044
1-800-456-4537
www.kohler,com

Kraft
306 E 61st
New York, NY 10021
(212)838-2214

Moen Master Brand Industries
25300 Al Moen Drive
North Olmstead, OH 44070
1-800-553-6636
www.moen.com

Pottery Barn
P.O.Box 7044
San Francisco, CA 94120
1-800-922-5507

PHOTO CREDITS

ABOUT THE AUTHOR

HELEN THOMPSON IS AN EDITOR, WRITER, AND PHOTO STYLIST FOR *METROPOLITAN HOME* MAGAZINE. HER WORK HAS ALSO APPEARED IN MANY OTHER PUBLICATIONS SUCH AS *COUNTRY HOME*, *TRADITIONAL HOME*, AND *RENOVATION STYLE MAGAZINES*. SHE IS THE AUTHOR OF *IN CELEBRATION*, A FOUR-BOOK SERIES ABOUT SEASONAL INDULGENCES. SHE LIVES IN AUSTIN, TEXAS, WITH HER HUSBAND CHARLES LOHRMANN.

ACKNOWLEDGMENTS

I WOULD LIKE TO THANK MY FRIEND AND AGENT BARBARA RODRIGUEZ FOR HER TIRELESS AND ENTHUSIASTIC EFFORTS ON MY BEHALF AND MY EDITORS MARTHA WETHERILL AND FRANCINE HORNBERGER, WHO HAVE BEEN GENEROUS GUIDES IN THE PUBLISHING PROCESS. LASTLY, I OWE A TREMENDOUS DEBT TO WRITER ANNIE KASABIAN, WHOSE WONDERFUL INTERVIEWS WITH CHEFS MADE THIS BOOK BETTER AND PROVIDE REAL INSIGHT INTO WHAT KITCHENS MEAN TO THE PEOPLE WHO USE THEM.